Thing Translator:

An Efficient Way to Classify Different Things

Thing Translator:

An Efficient Way to Classify Different Things

Rajat Ramesh Dungarwal
Vyom Makwana
Keyur Babariya
Vishakha Shelke

ELIVA PRESS

Published by Eliva Press
Email: info@elivapress.com
Website: www.elivapress.com

ISBN: 978-1-63648-372-6

© Eliva Press, 2021
© Rajat Ramesh Dungarwal, Vyom Makwana, Keyur Babariya, Vishakha Shelke
Cover Design: Eliva Press
Cover Image: Freepik Premium
Printed at: see last page

No part of this book may be reproduced or utilized in any form or by any means, electronic or mechanical, including photocopying, recording, or by any information storage and retrieval system, without permission in writing from Eliva Press.

Any brand and product names mentioned in this book are subject to the trademark, brand, or patent protection and are trademarks of their respective owners. The use of brand names, trade names, product names, product descriptions, is in no way implies that such names may be regarded as unrestricted by trademark and brand protection laws and thus may be used by anyone.

The opinions and views expressed are exclusively those of the authors/contributors and in no way the editors or publisher is responsible.

All rights reserved.

International Conference on Smart Data Intelligence
(ICSMDI 2021)

Table of Contents

Thing Translator: An Efficient Way to Classify Different Things

Mrs. Vishakha Shelke[a], Mr. Rajat Dungarwal[b], Mr. Vyom Makwana[c], Mr. Keyur Babariya[d]

[a]*Assistant Professor Department of Computer Engineering, Universal College of Engineering, vasai-401208, India*
[b]*Student BE Computer Engineering, Universal College of Engineering, vasai-401208, India*
[c] *Student BE Computer Engineering, Universal College of Engineering, vasai-401208, India*
[d] *Student BE Computer Engineering, Universal College of Engineering, vasai-401208, India*

1. ABSTRACT

Translation is the communication of a source-language text into an equivalent target-language text. A translator always risks in advertently introducing source-language words, grammar, or syntax into the target-language rendering. Thing Translator is an open-source offline application that uses the modern machine learning techniques – namely, computer vision and natural language translation. Thing Translator is a web app that lets you point your phone at particular object to hear it in a different language. The task of the translator here is to maintain a delicate balance between the source language and the language of translation. Thing translator is using Google's Translate API's and cloud vision as it was developed by Google as a part of AI experiment. The main reason behind building this application is to help each and every person to know different things in many languages and understand them better. When we want to travel outside our place or outside India then there may be difficulty that we may not know that language of that particular region, we find language barrier due to not understanding the language they speak there is also a language barrier if want to shop from another region. We have designed an application "Thing Translator: An Efficient Way to Classify Different Things" for every person to classify or recognize different things present around them. Thing translator is an android application which uses image recognition and object character recognition. This is useful to understand and to learn names of different objects just a capturing the image and also to learn pronunciation of the objects in native or other languages. This application can be used for the classification of necessary household objects present around us such as bottle, clock, facemask, wrist watch, comb etc. and also some electronic objects present in house that include laptop, television, charger etc. Also, we have included some flowers and animals.

Keywords — Thing Translator, Image Recognition, Object Character Recognition, Natural Language Translation and Text-to-Speech.

2. Introduction

Most of the times it is difficult for a person to know everything or knowing something in desired language. Sometimes it may happen like you the object in your native language but not in other languages so by using our proposed system it will be easy for every person to classify any object around you and learn them in desired language. So, by considering this difficulty google had built an app that scans the image and gives the labelled text and the desired output. Google and many such applications use Google's cloud vision API, so the primary requirement is internet connection, but most of the time at some place there is low or no internet connection and also there are some cases who can't even afford a stable internet connection. For them it is very difficult to use such android applications. Thing Translator-An efficient way to classify different things, is an offline system designed such that every person can make efficient use of it. This application is useful for students to learn new things. This will also help them in e-learning such as they just have to capture the image of the object in front on them and the model will classify the thing and will give a speech output in the desired language which the students want to learn. This application is useful for the students to learn pronunciation of the objects in various languages.

3. Literature Survey

The following research articles are selected for review, keeping in mind our project in the domain of Image Processing and Image Recognition. Table 1 shows survey of the research paper:

Table 1 – Literature Survey table

Sr. No.	Paper Name	Year of Publication	Author	Publication	Proposed Work	Research Gap
1	Text to speech conversion module.	2005	Hussain Rangoonwala, Vishal Kaushik, P Mohith, DhanalakshmiSamiappan.	SRM	This paper proposes a method at developing a complete system in which Text can be converted to Speech, Text file can be converted to Speech, Text in various Languages can be converted to Speech.	This research says that the device should have an internet connection and it cannot convert image into speech.
2	Character recognition system for cellular phone with camera.	2005	K.S. Bae K.K. Kim Y.G. Chung W.P. Yu	IEEE	This paper describes camera-based character recognition system, which is implemented for mobile devices such as PDA and cellular phones with color cameras.	This application is an online paid application as it uses techniques such as image enhancement and is only used for character recognition.

3	Sign Language Recognitio n, Generation and Modelling with application in Deaf Communic ation.	2009	Dr. Eleni Efthimiou, Research Director, ILSP/ATHENA R.C.	Dictasign	They post opinions, modify and enhance each other's contributions and share information.	This research was made only as a web application and it converts the sign signal into text.
4	A Guide to Translation Project Management.	2016	David Russi, Rebecca Schneider	Meted	This Guide to Translation Project Management provides a set of written guidelines meant to assist organizations around the world wishing to produce quality translations.	This research is only used for instructional materials used for training in NMHS's.
5	Translation technique of English abstract translation in journal edunomika.	2018	Tira Nur Fitria	Resear ch Gate	Descriptive qualitative is a method of research that makes the description of the situation or events or occurrences clearer.	This research is used only to find the translation techniques used in journal abstracts and to find out most dominant technique.

6	Food image processing techniques.	2019	S. Mohideen Pillai, Dr.S. Kother Mohideen2	JAC	As people across the globe are becoming more interested in watching their weight, eating healthier and avoiding obesity, a system that can measure calories and nutrition in every day meals can be very useful.	The research gap is only that it is not implemented as an android application it is limited only up to web application.
7	A Study on Text Recognitio n using Image Processing with Dataminin g Technique s.	2019	U. Karthikeyan, Dr. M. Vanitha.	JSCE	Text recognition is a technique that recognizes text from the paper document in the desired format (such as .doc or .txt).	The gap is only it is unable to remove the noise of the image signal.

8	Digital Image Processing- A Quick Review.	2019	R. Ravikumar, Dr V. Arulmozhi.	IJICT	Image is one of the evident sources in image processing applications. Image processing will dramatically change the human computer interaction in future.	This research is not yet implemented it's still only on the paper discussing about various image processing applications and techniques.
9	DEEP VOICE 3: Scaling Text-to-Speech with Convolutio nal Sequence Learning	2018	Jonathan Raiman and John Miller	IEEE Transacti ons	Deep Voice 3 is an order of magnitude faster than current neural speech synthesis systems when it comes to naturalness. Moreover, it exemplifies	The gap shows that the Deep Voice 3, a neural text-to-speech (TTS) system that is completely convolutional and attention-based.

10	Text-to-Image-to-Text Translation using Cycle Consistent Adversarial Networks	2018	Satya Krishna Gorti and Jeremy Ma	IEEE Transactions	It addresses this problem by employing a captioning network to caption generated images and exploiting the gap between ground truth and generated captions to further enhance the network.	The research gap is that they do not compare their approach to other methods in depth for better perspective of the method.
11	Direct Speech-to-Image Translation	2020	Jiguo Li, Xinfeng Zhang, Chuanmin, Jia, Jizheng Xu, Li Zhang, Yue Wang, Siwei Ma and Wen Gao	IEEE Transactions	The paper states that a speech encoder is specifically designed to represent input speech signals as an embedding function.	The research gap says that it should be trained with a pretrained image encoder using teacher-student learning to improve generalization capacity on new students.

| 12 | Visual Grounding in Video for Unsupervised Word Translation | 2020 | Gunnar A. Sigurdsson, Jean-Baptiste Alayrac, Aida Nematzadeh, Lucas Smaira, Mateusz Malinowski, Joao Carreira, Phil Blunsom and Andrew Zisserman | IEEE Transactions | The central concept is to learn embeddings from unpaired instructional videos narrated in the native language in order to create a shared visual representation of two languages | The research gap is that it does not aim to enhance unsupervised word mapping between languages through the use of visual grounding |
| 13 | FASTPITCH: Parallel Text-to-Speech with Pitch Prediction | 2021 | Adrian Lancucki | IEEE Transactions | Fastpitch produces speech by uniformly in-creasing or decreasing pitch. This is similar to voice modulation that is done on a voluntary basis | The gap is that the Fastpitch is a completely parallel text-to-speech model based on Fast Speech and constrained by fundamental frequency contours. |

14	SimulMT to SimulST: Adapting Simultaneous Text Translation to End-to-End Simultaneous Speech Translation	2020	Xutai Ma, Juan Pino and Pholipp Koehn	IEEE Transactions	While simultaneous text translation and end-to-end speech translation have made significant progress in recent years, little work has been done to combine these tasks.	By adding a pre-decision module, this project will investigate how to adapt wait-k and monotonic multi-head attention methods for simultaneous text translation to end-to-end simultaneous speech translation
15	Describe What to Change: A Text-guided Unsupervised Image-to-Image Translation Approach	2020	Yahui Liu, Marco De Nadai, Deng Cai, Huayang Li, Xavier Alameda-Pineda, Nicu Sebe and Bruno Lepri	IEEE Transactions	This paper proposes a novel unsupervised method based on image-to-image translation that changes the attributes of a given image using a command-like sentence.	The gap is that the proposed model does not separates image content from visual attributes, then learns to alter the latter using the textual definition before creating a new image from the content.

In the paper presented by Hussain Rangoonwala1, Vishal Kaushik2, P Mohit3, Dhanalakshmi Samiappan proposes a method for creating a complete framework that allows text to be converted into speech, text files to be converted into speech, text in different languages to be converted into speech, images to be converted into text, and images to be converted into speech, all while using the programming tool MATLAB. The various approaches are employed and then combined in an application for ease of use and accessibility [1].

In the paper presented by K.S Bae, K.K Kim, Y.G. Chung, W.P. Yu describes the camera-based character recognition system for mobile devices with colour cameras, such as cellphones. To begin, they created a computer-based camera-based recognition system that uses techniques like image enhancement and blob colouring to extract character regions and remove noise from camera-captured images. [2].

In the paper presented by Dr. Eleni Efthimiou, Research Director, ILSP/ATHENA R.C states the web has developed it has become a place where people interact. They post suggestions, modify and improve each other's contributions and share information. Dicta-Sign find the ways to enable communication between the Deaf individuals through enhancing the sign language based human machine interfaces [3].

In the paper presented by David Russi, Rebecca Schneider states the Guide to Translation Project Management is a series of written instructions designed to help organisations all over the world produce high-quality translations. While it was created as a resource for National Meteorological and Hydrological Services (NMHSs) to aid in technical and training growth, the general principles are applicable to any agency or organisation wishing to transmit information in other languages [4].

In the paper presented by Tira Nur Fitria states that the aim of the research is to classify different types of translation techniques and determine which one is best for journal translation. A descriptive qualitative design was used in this research. Descriptive qualitative analysis provides a summary of a situation, case, or occurrence, and this approach is used to gather basic data [5].

In the paper presented by S. Mohideen Pillai, Dr.S. Kother Mohideen2 describes that people all over the world are becoming more interested in keeping track of their weight, eating healthy, and preventing obesity. A device that can quantify nutrition and calories in day-to-day meals is very useful, and image processing is used in such systems to accurately identify food products. For food recognition, nutrient detection, and calorie calculation, image processing techniques such as image segmentation, feature extraction, object recognition, and classification are used [6].

In the paper presented by U. Karthikeyan, Dr. M. Vanitha states that the text recognition is a technique for extracting text from a document in the desired format (such as.doc or.txt). Pre-processing, segmentation, feature extraction, and classification are all stages in the text recognition process. The pre-processing is done to improve image enhancement while also lowering the noise signal in the input image signal. The segmentation process is used to segment the image provided online as well as each segmentation line character. [7].

In the paper presented by R. Ravi Kumar, Dr. V. Arulmozhi describes that in the image processing applications image is one of the most important sources. Image processing will change the human machine interaction greatly in future. A large variety of image processing applications and techniques helps to extract various complex features from the image. While nowadays image processing works so efficiently such that we can see what actually present in the image. Image processing is the real core from various techniques for image enhancement. This paper discusses the overview of an image processing applications, tools and techniques [8].

In the paper presented by Jonathan Raiman and John Miller states that the paper shows Deep Voice 3, a neural text-to-speech (TTS) system that is completely convolutional and attention-based. Deep Voice 3 is an order of magnitude faster than current neural speech synthesis systems when it comes to naturalness. Deep Voice 3 will scale up to dataset sizes never seen before in TTS. About two thousand speakers contributed over 800 hours of audio preparation. Moreover, it exemplifies [9].

In the paper presented by Satya Gorti and Jeremy Ma states that they compare their approach to other methods in depth for better perspective of the method. It addresses this problem by employing a captioning network to caption generated images and exploiting the gap between ground truth and generated captions to further enhance the network [10].

In the paper presented by Jiguo Li, Xinfeng Zhang, Jia, Jizheng Xu, Li Zhang, Yue Wang, Siwei Ma and Wen Gao states that it tries to convert speech signals to picture signals without going through the transcription stage. A speech encoder is specifically designed to represent input speech signals as an embedding function, and it is trained with a pretrained image encoder using teacher-student learning to improve generalisation capacity on new students [11].

In the paper presented by Gunnar A. Sigurdsson, Jean-Baptiste Alayrac, Aida Nematzadeh, Lucas Smaira, Mateusz Malinowski, Joao Carreira, Phil Blunsom and Andrew Zisserman describe Its aim is to enhance unsupervised word mapping between languages through the use of visual grounding. The central concept is to learn embeddings from unpaired instructional videos narrated in the native language in order to create a shared visual representation of two languages [12].

In the paper presented by Adrian Lancucki states that the Fastpitch is a completely parallel text-to-speech model based on Fast Speech and constrained by fundamental frequency contours. During inference, the model calculates pitch contours. By modifying these predictions, the produced speech can become more descriptive, better fit the semantics of the utterance, and, as a result, more engaging to the listener. Fastpitch produces speech by uniformly in-creasing or decreasing pitch. This is similar to voice modulation that is done on a voluntary basis [13].

In the paper presented by Xutai Ma, Juan Pino and Philipp Koehn describes While simultaneous text translation and end-to-end speech translation have made significant progress in recent years, little work has been done to combine these tasks. By adding a pre-decision module, this project will investigate how to adapt wait-k and monotonic multi-head attention methods for simultaneous text translation to end-to-end simultaneous speech translation [14].

In the paper presented by Yahui Liu, Marco De Nadai, Deng Cai, Huayang Li, Xavier Alameda-Pineda, Nicu Sebe and Bruno Lepri states that this paper proposes a novel unsupervised method based on image-to-image translation that changes the attributes of a given image using a command-like sentence like "change the hair colour to black." Unlike other methods, ours does not involve a human-annotated dataset or a textual explanation of all the attributes of the desired image, only those that must be changed. The proposed model separates image content from visual attributes, then learns to alter the latter using the textual definition before creating a new image from the content and the updated attribute representation [15].

4. Proposed System

To use this Thing Translator app firstly the user, have to place the camera of the device (cell phone/computer/laptop) in front of the object. Then it converts the raw object to the final image. Then finally the text is converted into speech using TTS (Text to speech) engine. Fig 1 shows the system architecture. In this the user will first select the language in which they want to know the name of the object then the user will have to capture the image of the object. The image of the object is now passed to the Thing Translator model which uses Convolution Neural Network (CNN) algorithm that is used to classify the image. In the model the image is then passed to CNN which creates the feature maps of the images and then the feature maps further pass-through multiple convolution layers which creates score maps and ROI's. Then it passes through the pooling layer and SoftMax activation function which provides a label to the image means text as the output. Then the text goes to Text-to-Speech module which converts the text into particular language which the user has selected in the beginning and finally the user gets the speech output of the image.

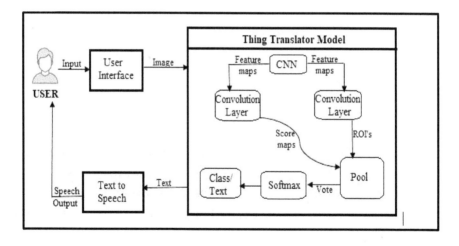

Fig 1. System Architecture of Thing Translator.

The modules are:

3.1 Image Processing and Image Recognition:

Image recognition/classification refers to the task of inputting an image into the neural network and getting a kind of label for that image as the output. The first layer of the neural network that is **"Convolution Layer"** takes in all the pixels within an image. After this all the data is fed into the network, then various filters are applied to the image, which forms the representations of the different parts of the image. The values that represent the image is further passed through the activation function after the feature is extracted from the image in the first layer. In this project we are using **"Rectified Linear Unit (ReLU)"**as an activation function that increases the non-linearity since images themselves are non-linear. After this it is further sent to the pooling layer, since there are various ways to pool the values but for our project, we are using **"Global Average Pooling"** to increase the accuracy. This pooling layer will keep only the parts of the image it thinks are relevant and removes the unnecessary parts. This pooling process makes the neural network more flexible and more adept at classification of objects/images based on relevant features.

4.1. Text to Speech Conversion:

A text-to-speech (TTS) system converts the given text on the screen into speech output when you press the convert button using the TTS engine in android studio. The Text-to-Speech (TTS) is also called as Speech Synthesis. This text-to-speech feature is majorly useful for the people who have the trouble reading the text displayed on the screen. The speech can be created by concatenating parts of recorded speech that is stored as the name of the object in the database. The Text-to-Speech engine enables the android device to speak the text in multiple languages. The Text-to-Speech (TTS) engine in the android studio platform support a variety of languages such as English, Chinese, Japanese, Korean, French, German and Italian. Fig 2 includes the block diagram of text to speech conversion module in the android studio.

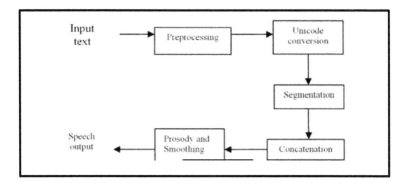

Fig 2. Block Diagram of TTS Engine.

5. Algorithm and Model

4.1 Algorithm:

The convolutional neural network (CNN) is a class of deep learning neural networks. Image classification is the process of taking an input (like a picture) and outputting a class (like "cat") or a probability that the input is a particular class ("there's a 90% probability that this input is a cat").

CNNs have an input layer, and output layer, and hidden layers. The hidden layers usually consist of convolutional layers, ReLU layers, pooling layers, and fully connected layers. Convolutional layers apply a convolution operation to the input. This passes the information on to the next layer. Pooling combines the outputs of clusters of neurons into a single neuron in the next layer. Fully connected layers connect every neuron in one layer to every neuron in the next layer. In a convolutional layer, neurons only receive input from a subarea of the previous layer. In a fully connected layer, each neuron receives input from *every* element of the previous layer.

A CNN works by extracting features from images. This eliminates the need for manual feature extraction. The features are not trained! They're learned while the network trains on a set of images. This makes deep learning models extremely accurate for computer vision tasks. CNNs learn feature detection through tens or hundreds of hidden layers. Each layer increases the complexity of the learned features[16].

A CNN

- Starts with an input image

- Applies many different filters to it to create a feature map

- Applies a ReLU function to increase non-linearity

- Applies a pooling layer to each feature map

- Flattens the pooled images into one long vector.

- Inputs the vector into a fully connected artificial neural network.

- Processes the features through the network. The final fully connected layer provides the "voting" of the classes that we're after.

- Trains through forward propagation and backpropagation for many, many epochs. This repeats until we have a well-defined neural network with trained weights and feature detectors.

For image recognition/classification, we are using TensorFlow and Keras. TensorFlow compiles of many different algorithms and models together, but for this image classification we use "Convolution Neural Network (CNN)" algorithm and "MobileNetV2" model. The CNN algorithm consists of various steps for image classification. The First step is the Input Layer which resets the data uploaded and allows us to set the batch size, in this project the batch size is set to 30. Then the second step consists of the convolution layer which takes in all the pixels within an image to create the feature maps that consists of the values that represent the particular image. These values are further passed in the activation function ReLU that increases the non-linearity of the images. The third step is to add the pooling layer, since there exist multiple types of pooling layer, we are using GlobalAveragePooling2D to reduce the size of the input and to increase the accuracy of the network. The next step is adding the dense layers in the network that will connect all the neurons and we added a different activation function that is SoftMax in this layer of neural network. The SoftMax function returns the probability and will output one value for each node in the output layer. The final step is the Logit layer which will take the output of the dense layer and then produce the raw prediction values.

4.2 Dataset:

A collection of images means the dataset is mainly required to train the neural network model. The dataset contains hundreds to thousands   of   sample images of objects for the Artificial Intelligence model to recognize them. The dataset contains 20,000+ pictures of 80+ different objects present that the people can see around them and recognize the object. The dataset is split into 0.8:0.2 ratio, where 80% of the total pictures is used for training the AI model and 20% to test the performance of the AI model as it is training.

4.3 Model:

There are various model types available, but in this application MobileNetV2 model is used to train the Artificial Intelligence model. MobileNetV2 is a convolutional neural network that is 53 layers deep. This MobileNetV2 model is a pretrained network that can classify images into different object categories. Fig 3 shows the different layers and model used in this algorithm.

```
model.summary()

Model: "sequential_4"

Layer (type)                    Output Shape           Param #
=================================================================
mobilenetv2_1.00_224 (Functi (None, 7, 7, 1280)        2257984

conv2d_4 (Conv2D)            (None, 5, 5, 32)          368672

dropout_4 (Dropout)          (None, 5, 5, 32)          0

global_average_pooling2d_4 ( (None, 32)                0

dense_4 (Dense)              (None, 32)                1056
=================================================================
```

Fig 3. Model Summary.

6. Fundamental Model and UML Diagrams

5.1 Data Flow Model

Data Flow Diagram (DFD) shows graphical representation of the" flow" of data through an information system, modelling its process aspects. It includes data inputs and outputs, data stores, and the various subprocesses the data moves through. DFDs are built using standardized symbols and notation to describe various entities and their relationships.

DFD LEVEL 0

Figure 4 denotes the Level 0 Data Flow Diagram of the proposed system. It is also known as the Context Diagram. This is the most basic representation of the system. It shows a data system as a whole and emphasizes the way it interacts with external entities. It is a complex representation of entire system. It displays the most abstract form of a system It gives a quick idea about the data flow inside the system. There is only one visible process that represents the functions of a complete system. The system for simplification is divided by three entities that make up the level 0 DFD i.e., User, Thing translator application and Tensor flow model. There is two-way communication between the user and Thing translator application. User will take the photo of the object he has to know about, then our system will send that image to the model made by us and then the model will send acknowledgement in form of label which will be converted as speech by the application using TTS engine and finally the application will give the output to the user.

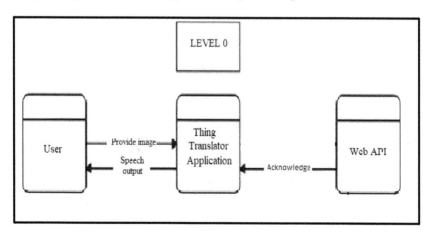

Figure 4 – DFD Level 0

DFD LEVEL 1

Figure 5 shows the Level 1 Data Flow Diagram of the proposed system. It is exactly the same as the Level 0 DFD, but much simplified. The Level 1 DFD shows how the system is divided into sub-systems i.e., subprocesses, each of which deals with one or more of the data flows to or from an external agent, and which together provide all of the functionality of the system as a whole. It breaks down the main processes into subprocesses that can then be analyzed and improved on a more intimate level. The DFD level 0 components are broken down into sub parts where Tensor flow model is divided into Training and Testing database.

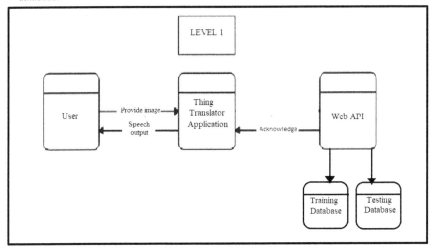

Figure 5 – DFD Level 1

5.2 Activity Diagram

In figure 6, we can observe the activity diagram. The four elements are capturing the image, detecting & cropping the image, classifying the image, labelling of image & speech output. Initially the application will capture the image and will check whether the image is clear or not and then the image will further pass for the detection process, if the image is detected properly then the application will classify the image and label it accordingly. Finally, the speech output will be given.

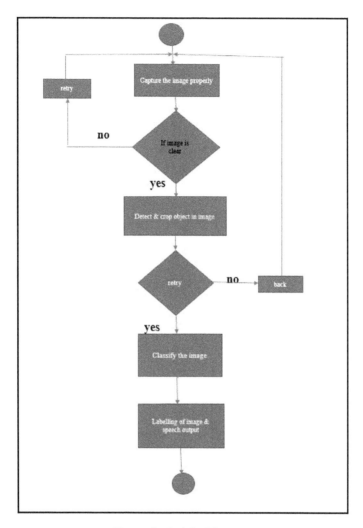

Figure. 6 – Activity Diagram

5.3 Sequence Diagram

In figure 7, we can observe the sequence diagram. The four elements are capturing the image, detecting & cropping the image, classifying the image, labelling of image & speech output. Initially the application will capture the image and will check whether the image is clear or not and then the image will further pass for the detection process, if the image is detected properly then the application will classify the image and label it accordingly. Finally, the speech output will be given.

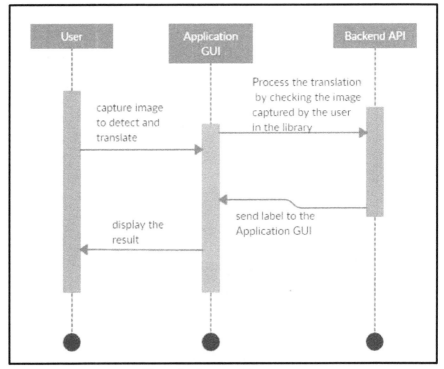

Figure. 7 – Sequence Diagram

5.3 Component Diagram

In figure 8, we can observe the component diagram. In Unified Modeling Language, a component diagram depicts how components are wired together to form larger components or software systems. They are used to illustrate the structure of arbitrarily complex systems. In our proposed system i.e., THING TRANSLATOR, the system will collect the image of the object captured by the user and further the image will be cropped accordingly. Then the model will analyses and detect the object and convert the image into text. The text is sent to the system then the system will convert the text into speech using TTS ENGINE and the result will be displayed on the screen.

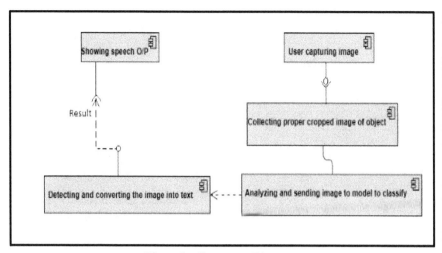

Figure. 8 – Component Diagram

5.4 Deployment Diagram

In figure 9, we can observe the deployment diagram. A UML deployment diagram is a diagram that shows the configuration of run time processing nodes and the components that live on them. Deployment diagrams is a kind of structure diagram used in modelling the physical aspects of an object-oriented system. They are often be used to model the static deployment view of a system (topology of the hardware). In proposed system i.e., THING TRANSLATOR there are two components client and server. The client component comprises of user wherein the image of the object will be captured using camera and cropped accordingly. The server component comprises of Thing Translator system and model. The cropped image of the object will be passed through the Thing translator model where the model will detect the object and label it accordingly. Then the labelled text will be given to the system where the text will be converted into speech using TTS engine and it will be displayed in data display system to the user.

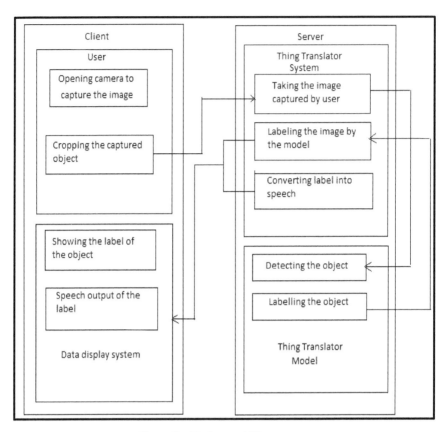

Figure. 9 – Deployment Diagram

7. Result and Analysis

5.1 Accuracy:

The efficiency of the project is based on accuracy. Accuracy is an important part of this project, majorly in terms of classification. It compares the classified image to the data source that is considered to be accurate data. There are many ways with which we can check whether the model is able to classify the image correctly or not and one of the ways of checking the accuracy is by graph. In CNN epoch refers to one cycle through the full training dataset and training the model takes more than a few epochs. There is no guarantee that the model will perform better by letting it learn the data for multiple epochs, so it is an art to decide the number of epochs that is sufficient for the neural network but in our case, it is 20. The accuracy of the system is above 85% - 90%. Fig 10 shows the accuracy on the train and test dataset. The graph is number of epochs vs accuracy. In this "Training and Validation Accuracy" graph the accuracy varies as the number of epochs are increased in the x-axis. The orange line in this graph shows the accuracy of the model on the train dataset whereas the blue line shows the accuracy of the model on the test dataset on which it is trained. The closer these two lines, the better is the model trained in the terms of accuracy. Epoch is performed to know the accuracy of the trained AI model. In this epoch there is val_loss and val_accuracy which helps us to know the accuracy obtained by the AI model.

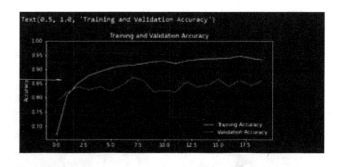

Fig 10. Accuracy.

The snapshots of the application and the actual outputs that were seen by the user. Below are the snapshots that include different pages of our application. Whenever you open the application, you have to first select the language in which you have to know the desired object. You can select only one language at a time, once you have selected the language then you have to click on the start button below. After clicking the start button, the application will open the camera to capture the object. Once you have captured the image after clicking on the start button on the first page, now you have to click on convert button. After clicking on the button, the application will classify the object that you have captured and will provide you the speech output and also the text in the particular language that you had selected in the first page. Also, there is a back button that will take you on the first page so you can again select the desired language and classify the object. Fig 11 shows the snapshots of UI that includes the select language page and the classify page. These figure includes some of the examples of the object that is included.

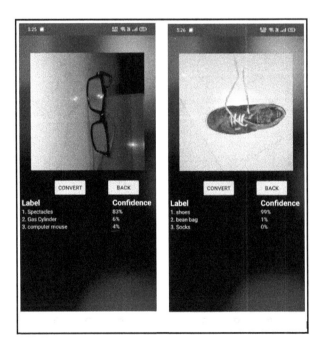

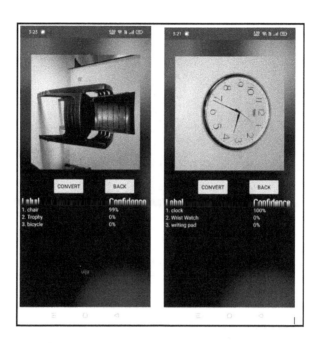

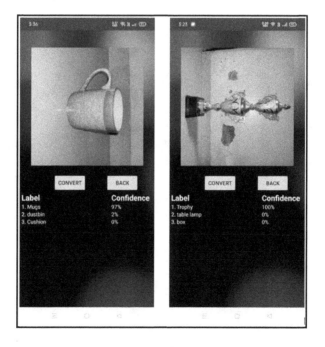

Fig 11. Snapshots of UI.

5.3 Result in Table:

Table 2 – Comparison between existing and
proposed system.

Parameter	Existing System	Proposed System
Internet connection	It requires internet connection to classify or detect objects as it is an online application	It does not require internet connection to classify as it is an offline application
API	The existing system uses Google's vision API developed by Google	The proposed system uses tensor flow model
Accuracy	The accuracy of existing system is more than the proposed system as it uses Google's vision API	The accuracy of proposed system is less than existing system
Speed	The existing system takes time to classify objects as it is an online application	The proposed system takes less time than existing system as it is an offline application

8. Conclusion

Most of the times it is difficult for a person to know everything or knowing something in every language spoken in the world. Our aim behind building this is: There are thousands of languages spoken in the world, and most spoken languages are English, Chinese, Japanese and Hindi so if we want to travel outside our place or outside India then there may be difficulty that we may not know that language of that particular region, we find language barrier due to not understanding the language they speak there is also a language barrier if want to shop from another region. So, by considering this difficulty google had built an app that scans the image and gives the desired output. This application will first convert the image into text and then text into desired language. This application will help many people to know the particular object in different language and also this will help to learn and understand their pronunciation better. This will also help in avoiding or reducing the language barrier when you are migrating to different place. We have built the offline application as there is not possible to have the internet connection everywhere. This application can only be used for the classification of necessary household objects present around us such as bottle, clock, facemask, wrist watch, comb etc. and also some electronic objects present in house that include laptop, television, charger etc. Also, we have included some flowers and animals. We still are looking for open-source ape to made a fully functional application which useful for all Indian peoples, so feel free to contribute.

9. References

[1] Hussain Rangoonwala1, Vishal Kaushik2, P Mohit3, Dhanalakshmi Samiappan, (2005), "Text to Speech Conversion Module", (SRM).

[2] K.S. Bae, K.K. Kim, Y.G. Chung W.P. Yu, (2005), "Character Recognition system for cellular phone with camera", (IEEE).

[3] Dr. Eleni Efthimiou, (2009), "Sign Language Recognition, Generation and Modelling with application in Deaf Communication", (Dictasign).

[4] David Russi, Rebecca Schneider, (2016), "A Guide to translation project management", (Meted).

[5] Tira Nur Fitria, (2018), "Translation technique of English abstract translation in journal edunomica", (Research Gate).

[6] S. Mohideen Pillai, Dr.S. Kother Mohideen, (2019), "Food image processing techniques", (JAC).

[7] U. Karthikeyan, Dr.M. Vanithal, (2019), "A Study on text recognition using image processing with datamining techniques", (JSCE).

[8] R. Ravikumar, Dr.V. Arulmozhi, (2019), "Digital image processing", (IJICT).

[9] Jonathan Raiman, John Miller, (2018), "DEEP VOICE 3: Scaling Text-to-Speech with Convolutional Sequence Learning", (IEEE Transactions).

[10] Satya Krishna Gorti, Jeremy Ma, (2018), "Text-to-Image-to-Text Translation using Cycle Consistent Adversarial Networks", (IEEE Transactions).

[11] Jiguo Li, Xinfeng Zhang, Chuanmin, Jia, Jizheng Xu, Li Zhang, Yue Wang, Siwei Ma, Wen Gao, (2020), "Direct Speech-to-Image Translation", (IEEE Transactions).

[12] Gunnar A. Sigurdsson, Jean-Baptiste Alayrac, Aida Nematzadeh, Lucas Smaira, Mateusz Malinowski, Joao Carreira, Phil Blunsom, Andrew Zisserman, (2020), "Visual Grounding in Video for Unsupervised Word Translation", (IEEE Transactions).

[13] Adrian Lancucki, (2021), "FASTPITCH: Parallel Text-to-Speech with Pitch Prediction", (IEEE Transactions).

[14] Xutai Ma, Juan Pino, Pholipp Koehn, (2020), "SimulMT to SimulST: Adapting Simultaneous Text Translation to End-to-End Simultaneous Speech Translation", (IEEE Transactions).

[15] Yahui Liu, Marco De Nadai, Deng Cai, Huayang Li, Xavier Alameda-Pineda, Nicu Sebe, Bruno Lepri, (2020), "Describe What to Change: A Text-guided Unsupervised Image-to-Image Translation Approach", (IEEE Transactions).

[16] https://towardsdatascience.com/wtf-is-image-classification-8e78a8235acb, "What is Image Classification and its steps".

Mrs. Vishakha Shelke received M.E Computer from Savitribai Phule Pune University currently working as an Assistant Professor and Project Coordinator in department of computer engineering at Universal College of Engineering, Mumbai. She has 11 years of teaching experience. Her area of interest is Machine Learning, Artificial intelligence.

Rajat Dungarwal, student at Universal college of engineering, Mumbai in department of computer engineering. Currently pursuing B.E Computer engineering from University of Mumbai. Worked as a volunteer in U&I organization for 1 year. His research interest includes Data science, Data analysis and Machine Learning.

Vyom Makwana, student at Universal college of engineering, Mumbai in department of computer engineering. Currently pursuing B.E Computer engineering from University of Mumbai. His research interest includes Machine Learning and Game Development.

Keyur Babariya, student at Universal college of engineering, Mumbai in department of computer engineering. Currently pursuing B.E Computer engineering from University of Mumbai. His research interest includes Artificial Intelligence and UI Designing.

Publisher: Eliva Press SRL

Email: info@elivapress.com

All rights reserved

Eliva Press is an independent publishing house established for the publication and dissemination of academic works all over the world. Company provides high quality and professional service for all of our authors.

Our Services:
Free of charge, open-minded, eco-friendly, innovational.

-Free standard publishing services (manuscript review, step-by-step book preparation, publication, distribution, and marketing).
-No financial risk. The author is not obliged to pay any hidden fees for publication.
-Editors. Dedicated editors will assist step by step through the projects.
-Money paid to the author for every book sold. Up to 50% royalties guaranteed.
-ISBN (International Standard Book Number). We assign a unique ISBN to every Eliva Press book.
-Digital archive storage. Books will be available online for a long time. We don't need to have a stock of our titles. No unsold copies. Eliva Press uses environment friendly print on demand technology that limits the needs of publishing business. We care about environment and share these principles with our customers.
-Cover design. Cover art is designed by a professional designer.
-Worldwide distribution. We continue expanding our distribution channels to make sure that all readers have access to our books.

www.elivapress.com

www.ingramcontent.com/pod-product-compliance
Lightning Source LLC
Chambersburg PA
CBHW070905070326
40690CB00009B/1999